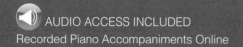
SINGER'S JAZZ ANTHOLOGY • HIGH VOICE

christmas standards

Arranged by Brent Edstrom

To access audio visit:
www.halleonard.com/mylibrary

"Enter Code"
3081-0766-7435-5445

ISBN 978-1-5400-9518-3

HAL•LEONARD®

Visit Hal Leonard Online at
www.halleonard.com

Contact us:
Hal Leonard
7777 West Bluemound Road
Milwaukee, WI 53213
Email: info@halleonard.com

In Europe, contact:
Hal Leonard Europe Limited
42 Wigmore Street
Marylebone, London, W1U 2RN
Email: info@halleonardeurope.com

In Australia, contact:
Hal Leonard Australia Pty. Ltd.
4 Lentara Court
Cheltenham, Victoria, 3192 Australia
Email: info@halleonard.com.au

ARRANGER'S NOTE

The vocalist's part in the *Singer's Jazz Anthology* matches the original sheet music but is *not* intended to be sung verbatim. Instead, melodic embellishments and alterations of rhythm and phrasing should be incorporated to both personalize a performance and conform to the accompaniments. In some cases, the form has been expanded to include "tags" and other endings not found in the original sheet music. In these instances, the term *ad lib.* indicates new melodic material appended to the original form.

Although the concept of personalizing rhythms and embellishing melodies might seem awkward to singers who specialize in classical music, there is a long tradition of melodic variation within the context of performance dating back to the Baroque. Not only do jazz singers personalize a given melody to fit the style of an accompaniment, they also develop a distinctive sound that helps *further* personalize their performances. Undoubtedly, the best strategy for learning how to stylize a jazz melody is to listen to recordings from the vocal jazz canon, including artists such as Nat King Cole, Ella Fitzgerald, Billie Holiday, Frank Sinatra, Sarah Vaughan, Nancy Wilson, and others.

The accompaniments in the *Singer's Jazz Anthology* can also be embellished by personalizing rhythms or dynamics, and chord labels are provided for pianists who are comfortable playing their own chord voicings. In some cases, optional, written-out improvisations are provided. These can be performed "as is," embellished, or skipped, depending on the performers' preference.

The included audio features piano recordings that can be used as a rehearsal aid or to accompany a performance. Tempi were selected to fit the character of each accompaniment, and the optional piano solos were omitted to provide a more seamless singing experience for vocalists who utilize them as backing tracks.

I hope you find many hours of enjoyment exploring the *Singer's Jazz Anthology* series!

Brent Edstrom

ALL I WANT FOR CHRISTMAS IS YOU

Words and Music by MARIAH CAREY
and WALTER AFANASIEFF

CODA

BLUE CHRISTMAS

Words and Music by BILLY HAYES
and JAY JOHNSON

THE CHRISTMAS SONG
(Chestnuts Roasting on an Open Fire)

Music and Lyric by MEL TORMÉ
and ROBERT WELLS

Straight 8ths

rein - deer __ real - ly know how to fly. And so I'm of - fer - ing this

sim - ple phrase __ to kids from one to nine - ty - two. Al -

though it's been said man - y times, man - y ways, "Mer - ry Christ - mas to

you."   you."

CHRISTMAS TIME IS HERE

from A CHARLIE BROWN CHRISTMAS

Words by LEE MENDELSON
Music by VINCE GUARALDI

FROSTY THE SNOW MAN

Words and Music by STEVE NELSON
and JACK ROLLINS

(There's No Place Like)
HOME FOR THE HOLIDAYS

Words and Music by AL STILLMAN
and ROBERT ALLEN

Oh, there's no place like home for the

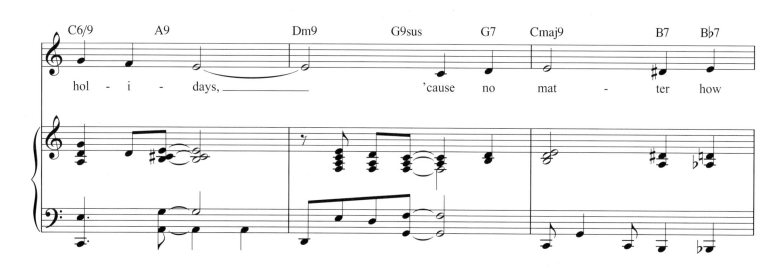

hol-i-days, _____ 'cause no mat-ter how

HAVE YOURSELF A MERRY LITTLE CHRISTMAS

from MEET ME IN ST. LOUIS

Words and Music by HUGH MARTIN
and RALPH BLANE

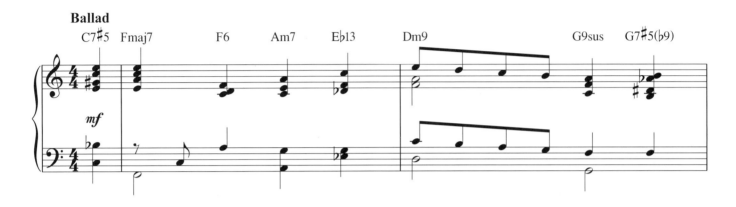

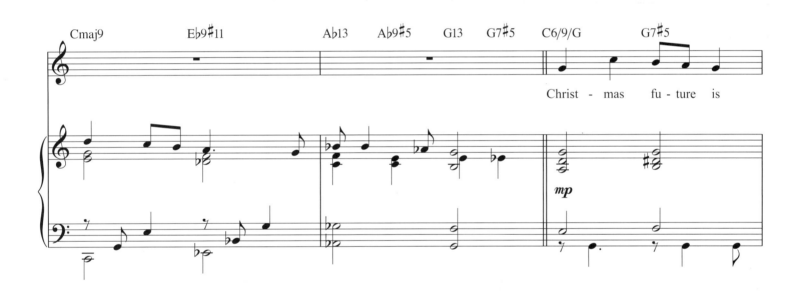

Christ - mas fu - ture is

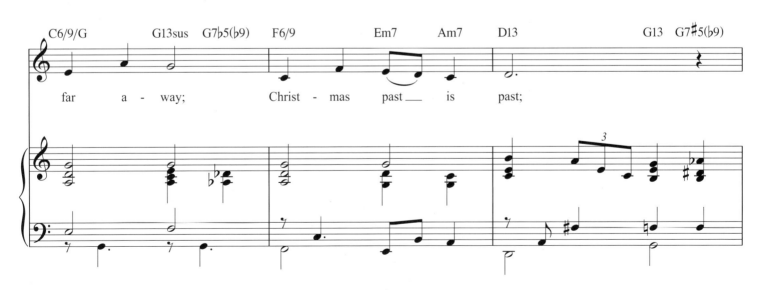

far a - way; Christ - mas past __ is past;

I HEARD THE BELLS ON CHRISTMAS DAY

Words by HENRY WADSWORTH LONGFELLOW
Adapted by JOHNNY MARKS
Music by JOHNNY MARKS

I'LL BE HOME FOR CHRISTMAS

Words and Music by KIM GANNON
and WALTER KENT

Gentle Swing

38

IT'S BEGINNING TO LOOK LIKE CHRISTMAS

By MEREDITH WILLSON

I'VE GOT MY LOVE TO KEEP ME WARM

from the 20th Century Fox Motion Picture ON THE AVENUE

Words and Music by
IRVING BERLIN

Bright jump Swing

The snow is snow-ing, the wind is blow-ing, but I can weath-er the storm. ___ What do I care how much it may storm? ___

LET IT SNOW! LET IT SNOW! LET IT SNOW!

Words by SAMMY CAHN
Music by JULE STYNE

A MARSHMALLOW WORLD

Words by CARL SIGMAN
Music by PETER DE ROSE

Moderate Swing

Lyrics:
It's a marsh-mal-low world in the win-ter _____ when the snow comes to cov-er the ground. It's the time for play. It's a whipped-cream day. _____ I wait for it the whole year 'round. Those are

MARY, DID YOU KNOW?

Words and Music by MARK LOWRY
and BUDDY GREENE

CODA

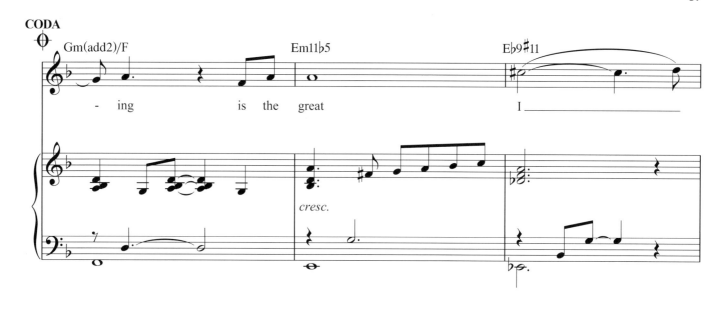

-ing   is   the   great   I _____

AM? _____

Freely

rit.

MERRY CHRISTMAS, DARLING

Words and Music by RICHARD CARPENTER
and FRANK POOLER

Rubato

Greet-ing cards have all been sent, the Christ-mas rush is through,

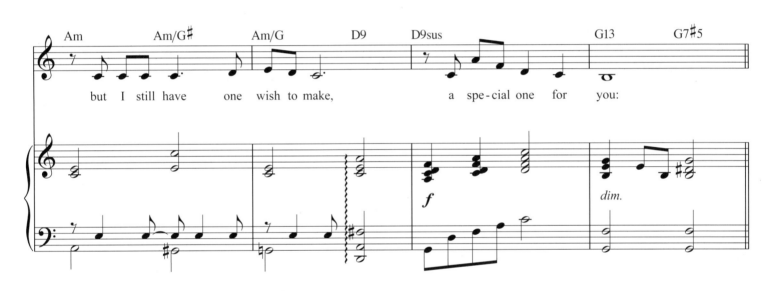

but I still have one wish to make, a spe-cial one for you:

Moderately slow

Mer-ry Christ-mas, dar-ling. We're a-part, that's true; but

60

MISTLETOE AND HOLLY

Words and Music by FRANK SINATRA,
DOK STANFORD and HENRY W. SANICOLA

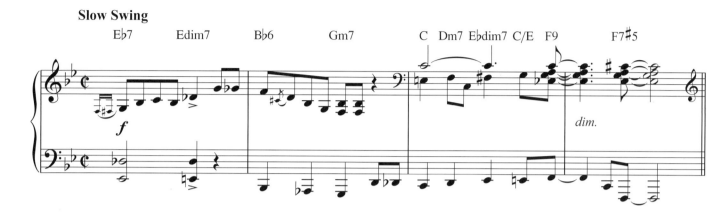

Oh, by gosh, by gol - ly, it's time for mis - tle - toe and
Oh, by gosh, by jin - gle, it's time for car - ols and Kris
Oh, by gosh, by gol - ly, it's time for mis - tle - toe and

hol - ly, _____ tast - y pheas - ants, Christ - mas pres - ents,
Krin - gle, _____ o - ver - eat - ing, mer - ry greet - ings
hol - ly, _____ fan - cy ties an' gran - ny's pies an'

coun-try-sides cov-ered with snow.
from _ rel - a - tives you don't know.

Then comes that big night, _____ giv - ing the tree the trim,

you'll hear voic - es by star - light _____ sing - ing a yule - tide

To Chorus   **D.S. al Coda** | **To Opt. Piano Solo**

hymn.
hymn.

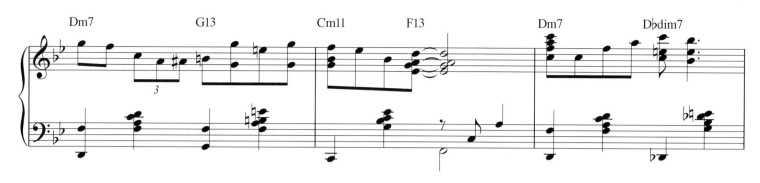

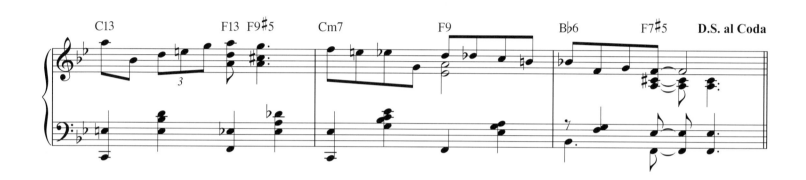

D.S. al Coda

CODA

folks steal-in' a kiss or two as they whis - per, "Mer - ry

cresc.

ff

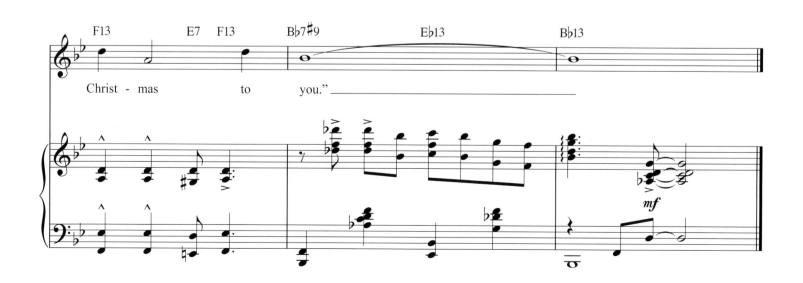

Christ - mas to you."

mf

THE MOST WONDERFUL TIME OF THE YEAR

Words and Music by EDDIE POLA
and GEORGE WYLE

Moderately, in 1

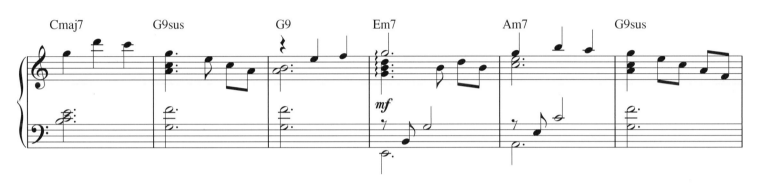

Swing 8ths

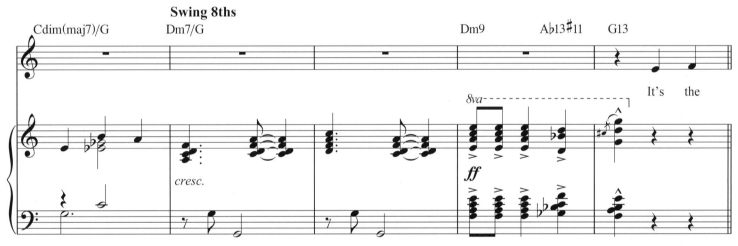

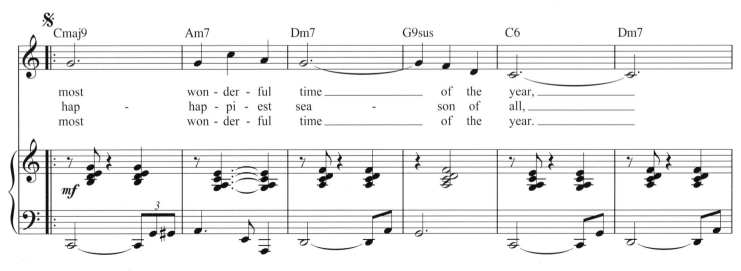

66

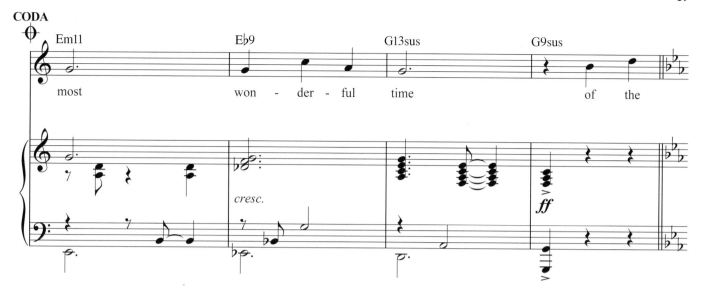

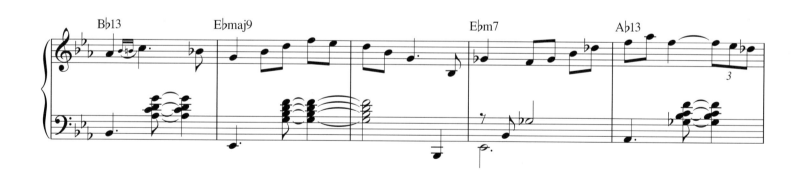

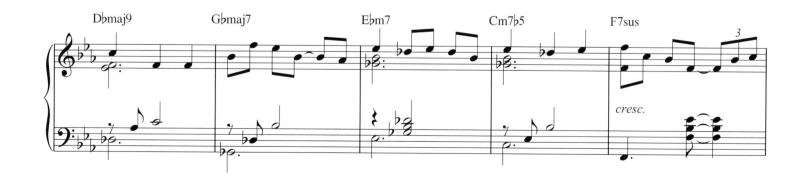

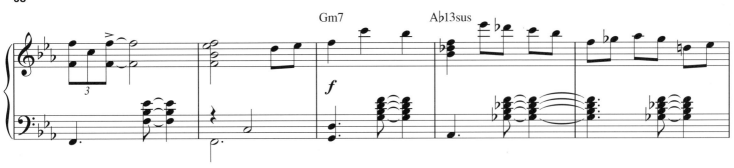

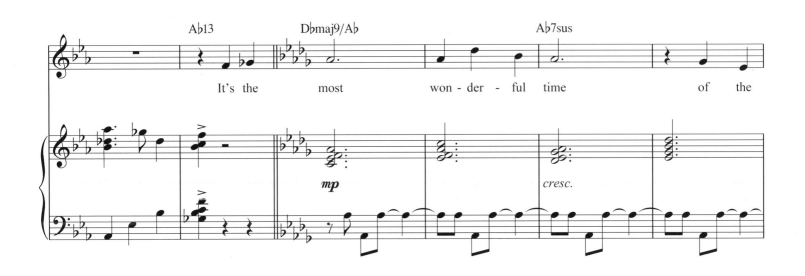

It's the most won-der - ful time of the

year._____ There'll be much mis-tle - toe - ing and

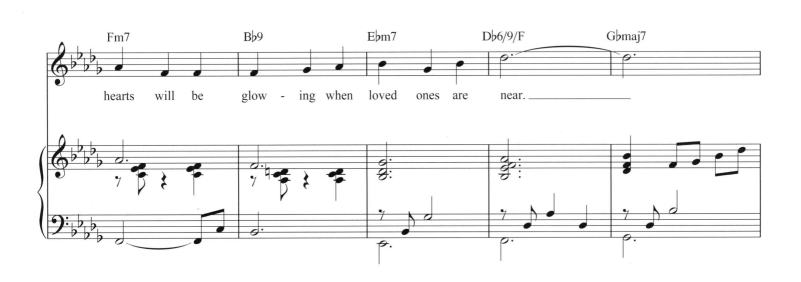

hearts will be glow - ing when loved ones are near._____

ROCKIN' AROUND
THE CHRISTMAS TREE

Music and Lyrics by
JOHNNY MARKS

72

RUDOLPH THE RED-NOSED REINDEER

Music and Lyrics by
JOHNNY MARKS

Then how the rein - deer loved him, as they shout - ed out with

glee: "Ru - dolph the red - nosed rein - deer,

To Coda

To Chorus

D.S. al Coda **To Opt. Piano Solo**

you'll go down in his - to - ry!" you'll go down in his - to - ry!"

you'll go down in his - to - ry!" _____

SANTA BABY

By JOAN JAVITS,
PHIL SPRINGER and TONY SPRINGER

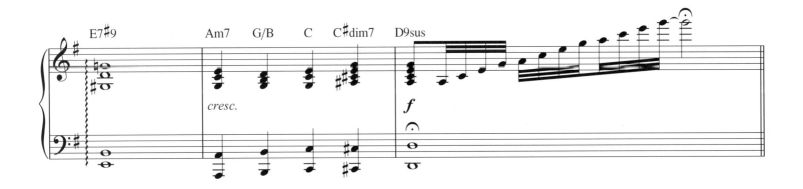

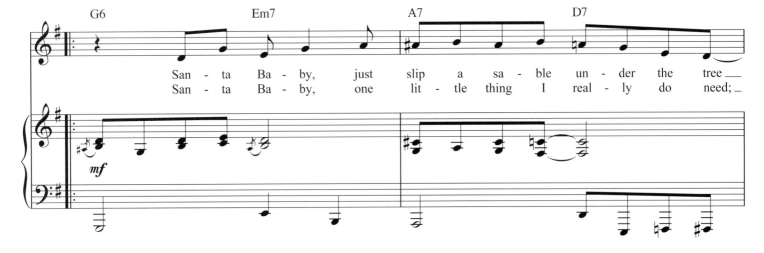

San - ta Ba - by, just slip a sa - ble un - der the tree ___
San - ta Ba - by, one lit - tle thing I real - ly do need; ___

SANTA CLAUS IS COMIN' TO TOWN

Words by HAVEN GILLESPIE
Music by J. FRED COOTS

Hard-grooving Swing

You bet-ter watch out, you

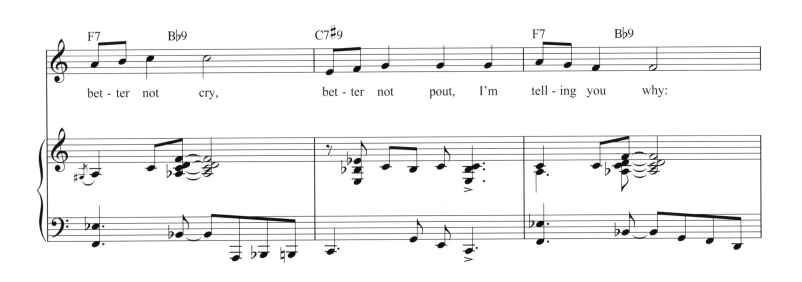

bet-ter not cry, bet-ter not pout, I'm tell-ing you why:

San-ta Claus is com-in' to town. He's

SILVER BELLS
from the Paramount Picture THE LEMON DROP KID

Words and Music by JAY LIVINGSTON
and RAY EVANS

SLEIGH RIDE

Music by LEROY ANDERSON
Words by MITCHELL PARISH

Moderately bright Swing

Just hear those sleigh bells jin-gle-ing, ring-ting-tin-gle-ing, too. _____ Come on, it's love-ly weath-er for a sleigh ride to-geth-er with you. _____

WHITE CHRISTMAS
from the Motion Picture Irving Berlin's HOLIDAY INN

Words and Music by
IRVING BERLIN

WINTER WONDERLAND

Words by DICK SMITH
Music by FELIX BERNARD

ORIGINAL KEYS FOR SINGERS

Titles in the Original Keys for Singers series are designed for vocalists looking for authentic transcriptions from their favorite artists. The books transcribe famous vocal performances exactly as recorded and provide piano accompaniment parts so that you can perform or pratice exactly as Ella or Patsy or Josh!

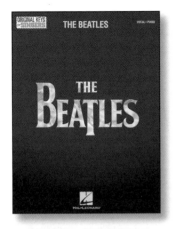  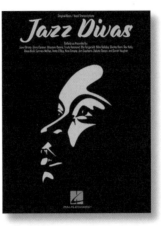 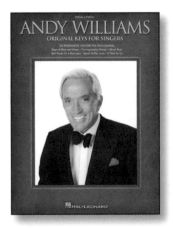